# Days to Remember

By Robert Gott

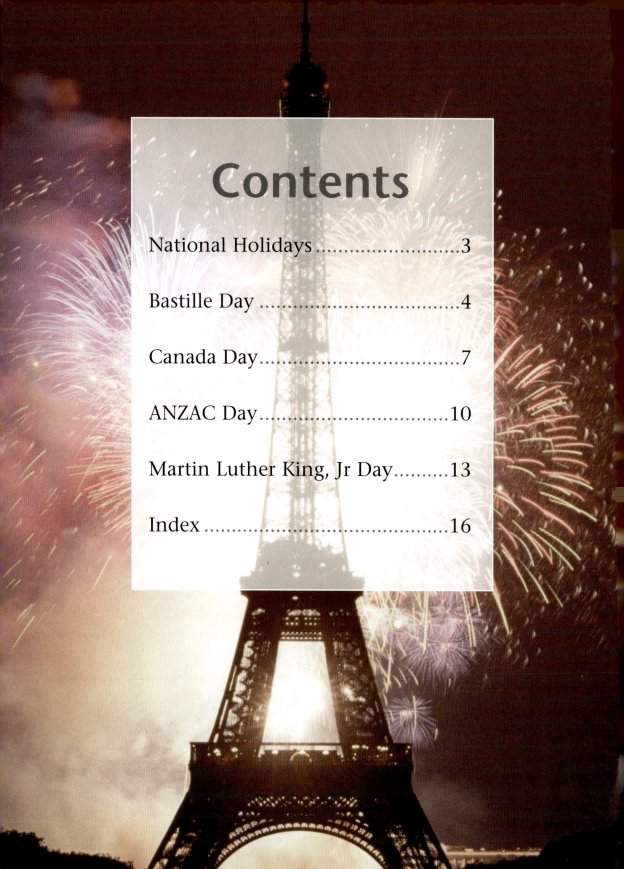

# Contents

National Holidays ........................ 3

Bastille Day ................................ 4

Canada Day ................................ 7

ANZAC Day ................................ 10

Martin Luther King, Jr Day .......... 13

Index ......................................... 16

# National Holidays

People celebrate national holidays all around the world. National holidays help people remember important events in the history of a country. Each national holiday has a story behind it.

ANZAC Day parade in Australia

# Bastille Day

## 14th July

During the 1700s France was ruled by King Louis XVI. He was very rich and enjoyed spending money. He made the people pay high taxes so he would become richer.

The people did not like the way the king spent their money. Many of them were poor and could not afford to buy food. Those who refused to pay taxes were thrown into prison.

After some time, the people joined together to fight the king and his laws. They planned to take over the Bastille prison because it was a symbol of the king's power. It reminded them of what could happen if they did not obey the king. On 14th July 1789 a large group of people forced their way into the Bastille and freed the prisoners.

Louis XVI was king of France from 1774 to 1792.

Aeroplanes fly over Paris. The planes' smoke trails are the colours of the French flag.

People crowd the streets to watch a Bastille Day parade.

This event marked the start of the French Revolution. The people killed the king and set up a new government. This new government was run by the people instead of a king or queen.

Today the people of France celebrate Bastille Day on 14th July. They have concerts, parades and fireworks. This holiday reminds them of their freedom.

# Canada Day

## 1st July

During the 1800s Great Britain ruled much of the land now known as Canada. It was made up of several colonies. People in these colonies wanted to form one country. They felt it would be easier to trade their goods and to farm the land if they joined together.

In 1864 people from some of the colonies discussed how they could form their own government. This project was called Canadian Confederation.

The British government agreed to the plan. On 1st July 1867 the colonies became a country called the Dominion of Canada. These colonies became the provinces of Nova Scotia, New Brunswick, Quebec and Ontario. Canada grew larger over the next hundred years. Today Canada has ten provinces and three territories.

◀ The Canadian colonists met in London to discuss uniting the provinces.

British Columbia was a British colony on the west coast. It agreed to join the Dominion of Canada if a railway was built to connect it to the rest of the country. The Canadian Pacific Railway was opened in 1886. ▶

Canada Day is celebrated on 1st July all across the country. There are concerts, fireworks and local events. Canada Day also celebrates Canada's Aboriginal people. Aboriginal people lived in Canada for thousands of years before other groups of people arrived.

The Canadian flag has a maple leaf.

Fireworks celebration in Ottawa, Ontario

# ANZAC Day
## 25th April

In 1914 Germany declared war on Russia, then France. Next they invaded Belgium. Then Great Britain declared war on Germany, and so World War I began.

Australia and New Zealand agreed to help. Soldiers travelled across half the world from Australia and New Zealand to fight in Europe and the Middle East. These soldiers became known as the ANZACs.

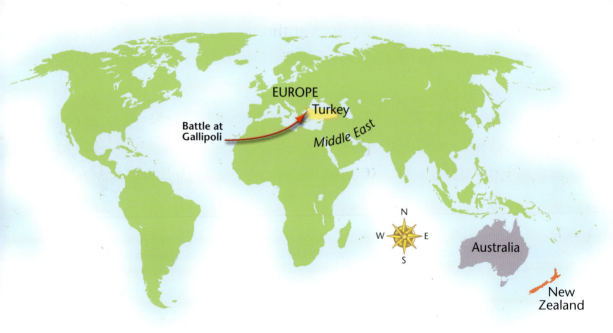

ANZAC soldiers travelled from Australia and New Zealand to fight in Europe and the Middle East.

Thousands of ANZAC troops landed at the Ari Burnu beach in Gallipoli on 25th April 1915.

On 25th April 1915 ANZAC soldiers landed in Gallipoli (guh-LIP-puh-lee), Turkey. At this time, Turkey supported Germany.

Many ANZAC soldiers were killed as they landed on the beach. They fought in terrible conditions for eight months.

Jack Simpson Kirkpatrick carried wounded soldiers out of battle on his donkey, Duffy.

On 25th April people in Australia and New Zealand remember the ANZAC soldiers. ANZAC Day services are held in cities and towns all over Australia and New Zealand. People remember how hard and bravely the ANZAC soldiers fought. Parades and picnics remember all of these heroic people.

Flowers are placed on memorials in memory of the Gallipoli soldiers.

Children remember their nation's heroes.

# Martin Luther King, Jr Day

## Third Monday in January

On the third Monday in January, people in the United States remember Martin Luther King, Jr. He was born in Atlanta, Georgia, in 1929. At that time, many states had laws that separated African Americans and white people. They couldn't eat in the same restaurants. They had separate water fountains, bathrooms and schools. Martin Luther King tried to change these unfair laws.

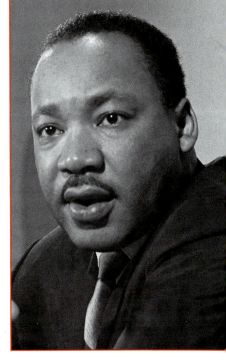

Martin Luther King, Jr

Martin Luther King, Jr was a powerful speaker.

In 1955 a woman named Rosa Parks was arrested because she didn't give her bus seat to a white person. Martin Luther King helped organise a peaceful protest among African Americans. They stopped travelling by bus until the law was changed.

Rosa Parks's bus protest inspired other people. ▶

◀ Rosa Parks today

Some people fought against Martin Luther King and others who worked for equal rights. He was arrested and threatened, but he never gave up. Tragically, he was shot and killed in 1968.

In 1986 the first official Martin Luther King, Jr Day was held. Schools and businesses now close all across the United States. There are services to remember his life and his dream. Today people try to make the dream of equality come true.

Many streets, schools and public buildings are named after King.

Today children of all races learn and play together.

# Index

Aboriginal people  9
ANZAC soldiers  10–12
Australia  10, 12
Bastille  5
Canada  7, 8, 9
Canadian Confederation  8
colonies  7, 8
concerts  6, 9
Dominion of Canada  8
Europe  10
fireworks  6, 9
France  4, 5, 6, 10
French Revolution  6
Gallipoli, Turkey  10, 11
Great Britain  7, 10
heroes  12
holiday  3, 6
King Louis XVI  4, 5
Martin Luther King  13–15
New Zealand  10, 12
parades  3, 6, 12
Rosa Parks  14
United States  13, 15
World War I  10